CURIOUS PEARL

SCIENCE GIRL

CURIOUS PEARL DIVES INTO WEATHER

An Augmented Reading Science Experience

by Eric Braun

illustrated by Anthony Lewis

PICTURE WINDOW BOOKS

a capstone imprint

CURIOUS PEARL
SCIENCE GIRL

Curious Pearl here!
Do you like science?
I sure do! I have all sorts of fun tools
to help me observe and investigate, but my
favorite tool is my science notebook. That's where
I write down questions and facts that help me
learn more about science. Would you like
to join me on my science adventures?
You're in for a special surprise!

Download the Capstone **4D** app!

- Ask an adult to download the Capstone 4D app.

- Scan the cover and stars inside the book for additional content.

When you scan a spread, you'll find fun extra stuff
to go with this book! You can also find these things
on the web at www.capstone4D.com using the
password: pearl.weather

Aaaaaah, feel the sun on your skin and the sand in your toes. There's no better place than the beach to read a science book.

"Come on, Pearl," said my friend Sabina. "Let's get in the water!"

"Can I finish this chapter first?" I asked. "I'm reading about weather."

"The weather is awesome right now!" Sabina said. "Why read about it when we can enjoy it?"

"I'm not reading about today's weather," I said.
"I'm reading about everything that makes up
weather."

"What makes up weather?" asked Sabina.
"Weather is weather."

I showed Sabina a page in my book. "Weather
is made up of a combination of things: sunlight,
wind, precipitation, and temperature. Wherever you
are, those elements are all present in some form.

They work together and give us different weather conditions."

"Well, they must be working together well today," Sabina said. "This weather is perfect!"

"They are for now!" I said. "But the elements can change, which will cause the weather to change. Sometimes very quickly."

As we waded into the lake, the sun reflected off the water into our eyes.

"Wow, it's bright," Sabina said.

"That's because there aren't any clouds," I said. "Clouds determine how much sunlight we see. If there are lots of clouds, it's not so bright."

"Actually, I see a few clouds," Sabina said. She pointed to the horizon.

"Eureka! That's a cirrus cloud!" I said.

"What's a serious cloud?" Sabina asked.

"Not serious. Cirrus is a type of cloud. There are four main kinds of clouds."

I pulled my notebook out of my bag to show her the four types of clouds. What? Don't you keep a notebook with you at all times?

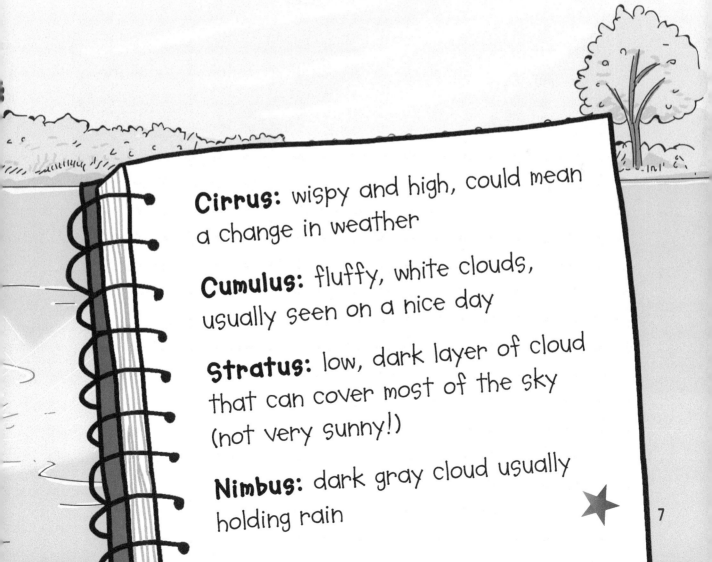

Cirrus: wispy and high, could mean a change in weather

Cumulus: fluffy, white clouds, usually seen on a nice day

Stratus: low, dark layer of cloud that can cover most of the sky (not very sunny!)

Nimbus: dark gray cloud usually holding rain

"Wind is part of weather," I said. "It can be still, breezy, or windy. Or really windy."

"Like that time when my homework got caught in the wind," Sabina said. "Remember?"

"We had to chase it for two whole blocks," I giggled.

"I wonder why some days it's windy, and others it's not," Sabina said.

"Let's look it up!" I said. We ran back to look in my weather book.

Cool air makes high air pressure, and warm air makes low air pressure. Warm air rises, and cold air falls. When the two meet, the differences in pressure make wind!

"This is my favorite weather," Sabina said. "Hot!"

"Temperature is another part of weather," I told her. "Temperature is the measure of how cold or hot it is. It's expressed as a number of degrees." I turned the pages in my weather book to the part about temperature. I made a note in my science notebook.

Temperature is measured on two main scales, Fahrenheit and Celsius. They both tell us the same thing, just using different numbers. For example, water freezes at 32 degrees Fahrenheit, but that's 0 degrees Celsius.

"Okay," Sabina said. "So there are clouds and sun. There's wind. And there's temperature. I forgot—what's the last part of weather?"

"Precipitation," I said. "That's how much rain or snow is falling."

"I'm glad it's not raining or snowing today," Sabina said.

I looked out at that gray cloud on the horizon. "Remember," I said, "weather can change."

"Why do you want to study weather anyway?" Sabina asked.

"Well, my book says that people measure all the parts of weather so they can notice patterns over time. That way they can predict what the weather might be like in different places at different times," I said.

"All right," Sabina said. "You said that weather can change. But I still don't get why anyone bothers studying it. We can't change it."

"No," I said. "But knowing ahead of time can be helpful. If you know what kind of weather is likely to come, you can make plans for the future. You'd know not to go camping when the weather is likely to be cold."

Just then, my little brother Peter's Frisbee landed in the water by us, so I dove down to get it. When I came back up, I tossed it back to shore. It landed next to Dad's umbrella.

"Why does your dad have an umbrella?" Sabina asked. "It's not raining."

"It's not raining now, but remember what I said about using weather patterns to predict weather? Dad and I looked at the weather report on the Internet this morning. The website said it might rain today."

Sabina looked up at those dark clouds she saw earlier. "They are getting closer," she said.

"Those are nimbus clouds," I said. "They carry rain."

"Let's get out of here," Sabina said. "I don't want to get rained on."

We ran up to shore just in time. It started pouring!

At home, we dried off, and I asked Sabina if she ever thought of moving somewhere with a different climate. "Climate is the range of weather that is typical to an area."

"Could we live in a climate that doesn't have much rain?" Sabina asked.

"Sure," I said. "The desert doesn't have much rain. But the temperature gets very hot. You might not like that."

"Hmmm . . . what other kinds of climates are there?" asked Sabina.

I grabbed my trusty science notebook to make a list of the five main kinds of climates.

Tropical: hot and humid; close to the equator

Arid: dry, like in deserts

Moderate: summers are hot and dry, winters are cool and wet

Continental: long, cold winters and short, hot summers

Polar: very cold for long periods of time

Dad reached over to grab our wet towels. "Every climate has certain kinds of severe weather," he added.

"Severe weather?" Peter asked. "You mean like hurricanes?"

"Sure," Dad said. "But we won't get hurricanes here because we don't live by an ocean. We know that hurricanes are not part of our climate. But we can get tornadoes and floods."

"Oh, no!" Peter said.

"Don't worry," I said. "We won't have a tornado or flood today. If something like that was coming, scientists would warn us. That's another reason why they study weather—so communities can be ready if severe weather comes."

Sabina and I did some research online and made a list of a few kinds of severe weather.

Thunderstorm: a rain storm with lightning and thunder; sometimes there's hail or severe wind

Tornado: a narrow, violent column of twisting air

Flood: when too much water flows onto land that is ordinarily dry

Hail: when thunderstorms produce frozen balls of ice

Sabina and I turned on the TV to see the weather forecast for tomorrow. It was good news. Another hot, sunny day means another day at the beach!

Meanwhile, Sabina had brought back some colorful rocks from the lake. We decided that a rainy day is a good excuse to do something different: make pet rocks.

Make Wind

Wind is created when hot air rises. Try this simple experiment to see how it works.

Here's what you need:

- sheet of paper
- pen or pencil
- scissors
- thumbtack
- short length of thread
- clothes hanger
- source of heat, such as a radiator or lamp turned upward

Steps:

1. Draw a spiral on the sheet of paper and cut it out.

2. Use the thumbtack to poke a hole in the center.

3. Push the thread through the hole and tie it on.

4. Tie the other end of the thread to the clothes hanger.

5. Holding the hanger, dangle your spiral a few inches above the heat source and wait.

Did the spiral start to spin? The reason is that the warm air rising from the heat source pushes it. This is the same way wind happens. Warm air rises, causing cooler air to be pulled to take its place.

GLOSSARY

climate—the range of weather that is likely in a particular area

cloud—a mass of water in the sky

forecast—a prediction about the weather

precipitation—water that falls from the sky; rain, snow, or hail

severe weather—dangerous weather that may cause damage, disruption, or loss of life

temperature—how hot or cold something is as measured in degrees

wind—moving air

READ MORE

Gerry, Lisa M. *Explore My World: Weather*. Washington, D.C.: National Geographic Kids, 2018.

Maloof, Torrey. *Extreme Weather*. Huntington Beach, Calif.: Teacher Created Materials, 2015.

Sohn, Emily. *Experiments in Earth Science and Weather with Toys and Everyday Stuff*. Fun Stuff. North Mankato, Minn.: Capstone Press, 2016.

INTERNET SITES

Use FactHound to find Internet sites related to this book.

Visit *www.facthound.com*

Just type in 9781515829720 and go.

Super-cool stuff!
Check out projects, games and lots more at
www.capstonekids.com

CRITICAL THINKING QUESTIONS

Describe the climate where you live. Be sure to mention weather for every season. What kinds of severe weather do you get?

What is an activity you've done or a trip you've taken that depended on the weather? How did you plan for this activity?

What is your favorite weather? Describe what all the parts of weather are like.

BOOKS IN THIS SERIES

INDEX

Thanks to our advisor for his expertise,
research, and advice:
Paul Ohmann, Ph.D.

Cover Illustrator: Stephanie Dehennin
Designer: Ted Williams
Art Director: Nathan Gassman
Production Specialist: Tori Abraham

The illustrations in the book were digitally
produced.

Picture Window Books are published by
Capstone, 1711 Roe Crest Dr., North Mankato,
Minnesota 56003
www.mycapstone.com

Library of Congress Cataloging-in-Publication Data
Cataloging-in-Publication information is on file
with Library of Congress.
ISBN 978-1-5158-2972-0 (hardcover)
ISBN 978-1-5158-2981-2 (paperback)
ISBN 978-1-5158-2977-5 (eBook PDF)

Printed in the United States   4430